T0129259

THE AFFLICTION OF EVOLUTION

Challenge My Empathy

LONNIE TROTT

authorHOUSE®

AuthorHouse™
1663 Liberty Drive
Bloomington, IN 47403
www.authorhouse.com
Phone: 1 (800) 839-8640

Published by AuthorHouse   03/29/2016

ISBN: 978-1-5049-8719-6 (sc)
ISBN: 978-1-5049-8717-2 (hc)
ISBN: 978-1-5049-8718-9 (e)

Library of Congress Control Number: 2016904867

Acknowledgements

Special Gratitude to my Power & Sustainer, Lord Jesus...

To my wonderful Mom & Grandmother; Mrs. Pamela Ben & Mrs. Loiuse Steede for stamping my Destiny, from a loving beginning.

Also, Warms Hugs to silent Angels; Miss. Laverne Griffin & Dr. Glenn Bascome, for who, Inspired and Dripped free will and Encouragement within my Hopes & Dreams.

To release and expose, to fall and arise stronger with direct conviction, watched and admired, many in my path. Those passionate voices not yet, motivated, I hear you. This is for All You Gems, before us, in front of us, that create, only what we Heart-fully wish...

NOT TO BE ALONE.

NOTE
(November 18, 2003, I took my most definitive building step, championing acceptance. Moving forward...)

Dear Dad   November 18, 2003

How are you? I hope and pray my letter reaches you in the best of, health, mind and spirit. Dad, first, I truly do not know where to start. yet I know that if I am to live a long loving and peaceful life with or without my family, I need to empty my most darkest emotions that I have allowed to eat and beat me down, by choice, because I wanted to believe that you truly loved me and honestly accepted me as your son. I am not talking about physical appearances, which by no doubt cannot be refuted. I am talking about mentally viewing me as a creation from your seed. About emotionally feeling and yearning to, and needing to know whom I am, as well as, feeling the loss of many years gone by. Knowing that they can never be regained, yet wanting to step out of pride and or guilt, so that you can't think of anything else but to find me, and hug me and allow me to hear your heartfelt words; "I love you son".

God...Dad, how I have ached, and cried, as I am at this moment, while writing, because I have felt so rejected by you. I used to ask myself why; why was I ever born. I would become depressed and wallow in self-pity, as I continued blaming myself for my mother and you not being together. Yes, I know that we have talked about this when you had come to see me. Wow! Nine years ago already, I am still hurting, mentally, people who I love because I am and have been holding you so high on my pedestal with my eyes close cause I had been too afraid to see the truth, reality. This is the main reason why I am writing this letter. I can not and will no longer allow myself to hold onto my one sided dreams for hope that you will one day hug me and tell me, your son, that you love me. I have hurt too many people that I love, and who I know genuinely love me, for too long; let alone myself. I am not getting any younger. I have a family of my own that I have forced suffering on because of the hold I had chosen to grip on you.

Yes, it could be said that I am my dad's son...though, today, I know that I am not you...I never have been. Nor, will I ever be...and inspire not to be. I need to be free to be me, myself. I need to stop messing with people's lives and emotions, owing to my greed, lust, and my selfishness.

I am and need to be individualized, for who I am. And that is Lonnie Eugene Trott, and not the son of my father, born in this world cause God expects me to express his love concerning my life and changes with in my life for the benefit of humanity, not self.

I thank God for so many good things too, out of feeling rejected by you. Curtis, your eldest grandson. I was surprised when you had come to see me years ago and you had told me that you remembered him, and you remembered his name. I was quite impressed, and then, even more hopeful for you and I. It took nineteen years for me to find Curtis, my son...Nineteen years! Even though my mom, "father", and everybody else said that, I was looking for my lost hope. Moreover, that if he wants to find me when he was old enough, he would. Yet, for me, that was not acceptable, and on my part, definitely not responsible. There was a cycle of how many years, God only knows, yet for my family, I was going to break the "neglecting father" cycle, which would help me to grow, as well. Over all, I am the parent, the adult. I need to take responsibility for my seed that bought an innocent life into this world. Moreover, more, to the truth, was hidden deep down in my soul was that I did not want to hold the label and or be like you, a deadbeat dad. You know, I used to despise the newspapers and the television programs, when I used to see the headlines, "Dead Beat Dads"...No! No! No! This was not going to be me. This is not who I am or will be, so help me God. I know now that I was, and I remain an innocent victim, concerning my conception. I had vowed that I was going to find my son, before I died. You know, I even wrote letters to the Oprah Winfrey Show, the Donahue Show, letters upon Phone calls and the use of the Internet, to locate Curtis. Nothing, and No-one, was going to deter me from my destiny.

Knowing I had and was neglected, you gave me a vital yearning to succeed. I do thank you for that. What was to be a joyous occasion for all, once I had found and talked to Curtis, for all that knew I was still looking for him, yet gave up on my favor of reaching my goal, was beautiful. Though, when I had called you to tell you minutes after I had hung up from talking to your eldest grandchild, you seemed more interested in returning to your bed, so I let you go. Dad, you know, you floored me. I thought, how insensitive. The one person that I had hoped would have been beside me; once again, you turned your back on me.

What is even more knife slicing, is that you have not once said anything to me, about or concerning Curtis. Not even, how is he doing. That morning at the Café in Hamilton, when you had came in and offered to pay for my bill; you did not even hint a thought concerning Curtis, your eldest Grandson. I have been waiting for you to say something. What Have I Ever Done To You!!! Nothing... Absolutely Nothing...Nothing more, nothing less...

I love my brothers and my sisters. Even though they are scattered all over Bermuda. God had his way for us to meet and to bond, instantly. When we talked, we all had the same pains, concerning you, our biological dad. Besides...My precious young sis, dad, I need to have you aware of another painful secret that I have never mentioned to any one, but God. I have envied and I have been extremely jealous of the relationship you shared with my sister. Though, it was good hearing you talk about her God given accomplishments, when you and I had run into one another in Hamilton at times; when I would listen to you, it would seem, to me, that you prided yourself on the things that you did for her and with her and my nephew, her son. You almost sounded like you were trying to force acceptance from me for abandoning the rest of "your" children and Grand children. Also, some of those times, I have to say, that, I pitied you. You would just gloat over and over...and dad, though I never once thought that you were intentionally trying to hurt me when you talked about going to visit her, which at times seemed three to four times a year, you were. You would go on about how you got her a car and an apartment. Than you would inform me, that she needs this and she needs that; and than again, you were going up to help her move into another place that you had got for her. Wow! Then the icing on the cake; the Time-sharing you brought for the two of you. Dad, what was I suppose to understand from that; and what the hell were you trying to tell me? What about the rest of your children? What about me, Lonnie? I had longed for your awareness of me, for many years of my life. There have been serious times when I had gotten myself into trouble and I had called you to helping me to acquire an Attorney. My family, on my mother's side, was gathering funds to afford a Lawyer, though you would not assist; not even put a dollar towards it. I felt so let down again, though I never verbally showed it.

I was twenty-three years old. A three-year infant trapped in my adult body, screaming for the one person in my life that could have made a world of a difference to me. You, for once, being by my side, unconditionally, under any circumstance.

In one sense, as I reflect on my own actions and my reasoning before them, I easily acknowledge and accept responsibility for my selfish self-centeredness. I only wanted, sought out, and accepted what would and could benefit me, Lonnie. You know what, I need to have you aware of something that I did not appreciate you saying or shouting out at our Wedding reception; yet, it was not until I had viewed my wedding video that I recalled you saying something and people laughing at it. It was so hypocritical of you. The nerve, to shout that out in front of my family and friends, let alone my Father, George, for all that matters; when I was giving my ceremonial speech to my wife, you shout out, "That's my boy!" I was your boy? As if, you had something spectacular to do with my wife and my present moment, besides sleeping with my mother. That was not right for you to do or claim, and I did not appreciate it. Over all, today, I still and will forever, love you. From God and from with in my soul, I forgive you. I am moving on, from strength, stronger, and evermore focused on reality.

Dad, still, you just have never been there for me. I do not even know what a hug from you would feel like. However, I am very interested; I am still moving on.

Out of all that's been going on, if there's one thing, one wish I could, and would ask of you - I am tearfully emotional at this moment – is, would you please, please look out for Marilyn and KC, my family for me. I have stressed Marilyn out, and she is pregnant and due in February, next years. I am here...I am unable to help my family, financially. She is hurting terribly dad. I have let her down horribly. I have let her down so hard. She says that I am her whole world, here in Bermuda. Now, she feels lost. You know, she was in the Hospital last week for three days, because of bleeding. The Doctors say her Placenta is too low. The Doctor has sent her home to total bed rest; which means she is unable to work until after our baby is born. Then after that, only God knows how long.

Dad... I need to ease the burdens I have forced upon my family, and to get my needed responsibilities back on track. Dad, I hope, all that I have released, has not disturbed you to much. However, I needed it. We needed it. I need to get on with my future with my mind clean and open, and my spirit free. And dad, you needed to know of the affects that I have allowed myself to be haunted by, confused by, and the hurt and pain I have caused innocent individuals, over many a years, because I was afraid to open up and see me, and to view my own, personal, story.

I, genuinely, do love you. Now I can, and will, breathe...
Happy Holidays... Take care... YOUR SON, LONNIE...

I've always been concerned with what makes our mind function in the form of thought. Is it possible to believe we are the thought of our ultimate function? Just the words alone give off an urge for challenge. Can we truly say that to know our true destiny in life is to know Immortality, first hand?

Family

05-29-91

If you could see me now,
What would you see?
For I'm looking at you,
My mind is in misery.
Here's what I feel.
Is my suffering showing?
Why, when I look at you,
You smile?
You're glowing!
Today's my graduation
And I'm lost!
Can't you see?
I'm trying... I can't focus...
Thank God, and my family.
Although our separation's painful,
Always remember this:
If you keep loving me,
You keep me loving.
To be needed
Is the key curing ...
Curing all suffering!

LONNIE E. TROTT

Cater – Cousins

1992

It's been too long -
To long since we met, last.
When will we join next?
Rejoin steadfast.
As you will to read me
I'm willing you in kind;
Two pure hearts,
Compatible with needs;
Yours and mine.
Oh! There's no love lost,
Though I'm blinded by sorrow.
Because you are the one,
My mind, my body...
My tomorrow.

LONNIE E. TROTT

The Picture

1993

After close to one year,
I can't believe you're here;
Wanting you so badly;
Bars separating our touch.
And knowing you realize my love holds much.
You're always a vision.
Did you know that, my dear?
Hey, yet it won't be long,
Till you are in my arms
Truly; heart fully; and
Sincere.

LONNIE E. TROTT

Focus

1993

Too, am I a tree?
Leafless in all my splendor.
I am lost, to a knight...
The freedom of my soul.
Am I the strength, so tall?
The Sky calls my crown to flight?
It was a tear; not the fear of losing...
My heart's my root... life's eternal soul.

LONNIE E. TROTT

You You

03-20-94

You You...
How I treasure knowing.
Our days are short...
Minds forever long;
Because of You;
Once dim and lost has breath.
Yes!!! I'm glowing!
You you...
My words never pass;
On a day as this day
Many years gone.
So many memories
Too few dreams remain as such
For as much; as to touch
A light that will last.

LONNIE E. TROTT

Where's The Light?

06-06-94

Once my friend; as a flower to a bee,
In my eye, so full, so lonely for sight.
Over years my mind longs, not just to know
But, to see... cause with the other eye,
The balance of hope that will keep;
My tears as honey... to a friend might.

LONNIE E. TROTT

Endurance

07-04-94

Every day is not the same;
I awake; eat; then sleep another,
Ticking hours, passing by; I want; I have;
I, I know my own power,
So many minutes; what am I to do?
Can I make tomorrow come?
Will I awake; will I?
It takes just a second; not even that:
To feel; cry; or to hurt.
But knowing you are liked
Holds time in a bottle.
I know,
I know,
I Thank You.

LONNIE E. TROTT

Reality

08-09-94

The finest of things,
Holds nothing less than beauty.
Yet, within a liquid;
Minerals and nutrients
Possess a stream of energy,
Combined, they form a solid,
Like breathing; life's' greatest gifts...
Individually.

LONNIE E. TROTT

10.

Tipped

08-09-94

Just a little bit of sugar,
Pour in the right amount of wine;
Your kiss could not be sweeter,
Nor cherished lips, so full, next to mine.
Oh Yes! Your heart is in the right place.
I will fill you with gallons of gore.
Do you know? You could've been my anchor?
Cause when I think of you, I want you, that much more.

LONNIE E. TROTT

Foresight

08-11-94

To fully enjoy the sun;
One must know or have an idea,
Concerning its rewards and meanings.
In pursuing and nurturing these rewards
One should be aware of the purpose;
For which such Joy and fulfillment
Has been bestowed upon them,
In support of your happiness,
Be the champion you are;
And you'll shine a ray
Of everlasting pleasure;
Enhanced with knowledge.

LONNIE E. TROTT

12.

A Chance

08-13-94

Two different worlds;
So many commons.
Only takes one chance;
Connecting communications to grow.
It's not a plea, demand or a summon;
Just two sides divided by elements;
Not much a task, No!
Just a bridge; but in this case;
A Pen; a piece of paper and an envelope.

LONNIE E. TROTT

Evolution (1)

09-09-94

The sun will be shining;
Though the smell of rain's in the air.
Your smile holds the scale of truth;
Those eyes I long to surrender.
In all the seasons we treasure a new;
For when the clouds wander,
A grey sky, turns blue.

LONNIE E. TROTT

Evolution (2)

09-09-94

Life is full of wonder,
As our senses pour hope into the valley of our fears.
Should your balance start to tilt
And the shutters fall short of September,
Always remember...
I Am Here.

LONNIE E. TROTT

Evolution (3)

09-09-94

It'll be winter, come October;
Yes, it's going to get cold.
Under the covers,
Your toes will seem brittle;
Not like ice, next to mine.
As we embrace one another.
For soon it will be springtime;
Then sunshine; your smile.
And hopefully, just hopefully,
Come summer, In a New Year;
My tears; your fears;
In the waters, through the valley,
Gone Bye.

LONNIE E. TROTT

Precious 70ᵀʰ

09-09-94

You know how much I Love You, you know how much I care.
You're in my life for always; the good, bad, and unknown.
You are my rock; the center of my world.
When I was a brat; I was loved; I was cracked; I was your star.
Though in my teens I came to know, all that was given
Was from your heart; that inner glow.
As I became legal; Twenty-one, as they say,
You Stood by your virtues and all your goodness, let's pray:
Lord keep this gem, a jewel of radiant beauty;
Her tongue is Wise... arms a blanket of warmth;
Oh God I Pray; My Sweet Grandmother's smile;
Her touch in every way.
Great spirits...
Truth and love anew.
My love;
My world;
The Air, which I Feed.

LONNIE E. TROTT

17.

Perfection

09-09-94

No! I'm not a bird;
Though I can soar in a vision.
I'm not a spirit;
Yet goodness compels in my soul.
I'm not white;
Though I've been stigmatized as a man of color;
Although, my eyes... colorless.
United with the universe with an open mind.
Guided by the light of truth;
Is knowing that the elements
Into our friendships endorsed...
By The Angels.
Though I'm not a man to confess
That the Word of The Bible's
My true understanding.
For, as you see; get to know;
And accept me as a being,
Is to Fly...

LONNIE E. TROTT

18.

Unsettled

10-12-94

There's that chill in the air;
Like the burning of a truth stand.
As I peak out my window;
Hoping, praying that what I feel
Is a reoccurrence of twelve months gone?
Dressing back, I fall into bed tied to two blankets,
A bed suit, and my woolen footwear.
OH that sound! Is that whistling a calling?
A calling to thou ears alone? Am I so worthy?
Do I not breath, taste,
Strut in the same light as my brothers' walk?
Why do I feel so eerie; so ghostly?
In a house with no structure; yet very cold?
Am I here; am I alive?
Why do I speak smoke?
Hello... hello...?
The whisper of thy heart's
As that to the shattering,
Of Ice.

LONNIE E. TROTT

What, Where, To Why & How

10-13-94

Through the window a vision of life.
From the mind;
Controlling the least of graphic detail.
The size, the hue,
Has nothing to hold one's Imagination,
Lest, that glimpse maybe the answer.
Just knowing,
A picture enhances a thousand meanings...
Is still short from the tree.
Its fruits; forever feeding,
Our perception,
With knowledge.

LONNIE E. TROTT

Life

10-14-94

Can you see that the ride is almost over?
All your foes and woes displayed for The Judgement.
The force which compels your sparks;
Your every breath's at doors end.
The light, the white light's calling...
If, if I could... I would..., I should have... What?
If to spare me a day so my repentance be abed...
I would...
Should tomorrow bring me more than Just?
I'm content with what's been given.
Allowing thy heart to exude thy precious gifts;
That jewel to forgive; show love in abundance,
Then rest...
A peaceful,
Definitive,
Sleep.

LONNIE E. TROTT

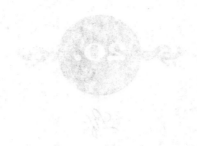

21.

Forgiveness

10-15-94

The thunder's a crackling
My last piece of salvation.
I'm in need; In need of a savior...
I'm willing your test.
What avenue has thou opened?
Opened for a son who knows
The value of thy love an understanding?
Can I bleed...? Will I ever know glory? Will I?
My heart's so full...
To accept a drink's to anticipate;
My past;
My present;
My unknown future,
With which all redemption's a blessing...
Consumed, within my soul.

LONNIE E. TROTT

Yes & No

10-15-94

Is the "sane" psyche an off-shoot of those?
Whom one would stereotype, insane?
How can one know, the hot from the cold?
If not for some form of force,
Compelling a chain reaction
To bring about the evolution?
Is not a day, a day...?
Lest, the stormiest of forces
Bring about the shadow of night,
Still that day?
I surmise, that we the "sane",
Fear that which understanding
Inflicts a border of superiority,
In so far, as to sustain the ideal being,
For which we the "sane"
Are no more In touch with reality
As our so called "insane "brothers and sisters.
They laugh at us... And we at them;
Yet, in Our Father's Eye,
We all are harmonized, as equals...
With Fellowship.

LONNIE E. TROTT

41

23.

Try Something Divergent

10-17-94

Tell a friend, about your Cous;
How much you love and care.
He's very cute...
Be up front, as to why I am here.
Cause an open mind serves healthy foods
No matter who does the deed.
For two consisting pens hold knowledge;
Though with understanding,
Our souls can't be breached,
To bleed.

LONNIE E. TROTT

Soul Searching

10-17-94

Will the strength of the elements ever be justified...?
In their destructive wake? All hearts are reaching for debris;
Not the sign! Lest, that thought falls short to suspect.
Fear not, vibes thy inner self,
For the shattering shall surpass all wayward Ill.
Take hold of substance; accept no not yours, but what's afflicted...
For the choice has lost respect,
In thy conviction.

LONNIE E. TROTT

Awaken

10-17-94

So many bolts, in the space of one hand.
No matter how vague; my hearts rains scarlet.
I've longed for a new; lost my past to yesterday.
Fangs I feel; an energy to release.
Why!
Why?
Why must a re-run hold my step?
Just a Sore and a biter soul...
Thy brutish needs sleep.

LONNIE E. TROTT

26.

Which Way

10-17-94

I want to run like the cat, on all fours;
I catch the hills peak. My thoughts as a river;
Flows many way too; and too fast to mention.
All my wires held by fuses; my pulse suffocating my air...
Should I be tested? Should I be tested so?
The answer...
The answer's to kind.

LONNIE E. TROTT

27.

Home

10-19-94

Never a dream so vivid, my mind shines anew.
So many memories; the bonding with pictures;
My Family.
The strength of my heart feeds...
I pump life within me every day.
Just knowing you care. It's true;
We're all housed in the assembly with God...
To stay.

LONNIE E. TROTT

28.

Diablo's Misfortune

10-25-94

He's up in a tree,
All my troubles held within good reason.
The olive tree bears fruit. A taste for comfort;
My negative side at rest. He can't get down.
Praise God!!
The world be gone from his grasp.
Let the roots stand firm, shoot the stork.
Above soar the sky; let him stay; let him stay...
Up in that tree,
Way up!
Way hi.

LONNIE E. TROTT

Lean On Me

10-27-94

Allow me to carry all your suffering;
My precious... My friend;
The vent for which we gave life;
Our Siriya.
I've so longed, for to hold... To touch...
Two, too many times I've reached out;
To your vision.

LONNIE E. TROTT

Personality

10-31-94

As I sit:
My mind's in a world of choice;
Thoughts and visions, flow in abundance.
Such a peaceful place, to sit all alone.
Not a care or the fear of losing... Not a care.
As I sit:
Like thunder... My hemisphere rolls;
My clouds weep, hot flashes...
As lightning; I'm spinning...
Sometimes praying for a rainbow.
Then just, when the sunrises...
That gloomy feeling regains its force;
All my dreams shattered, then I flush...
My ambiguous, weather.

LONNIE E. TROTT

A Particular Thing

10-31-94

How do I grasp, what does not exist;
Yet, in my mind, I control... It?
This one tell many yet few!
No, I'm not alone...
It's, my every comfort.
What?
What!
What I hold's not a secret.
What my thoughts fancy cannot wander.
I want to ponder. I want to tell...
Speak to... Explain to... Yet it's just...
It.

LONNIE E. TROTT

32.

Something Else

10-31-94

Something inside... A point.
Questions the agony of my woes!
No answer; No cure; with in my structure?
Sooo hollow; Hum... Something inside... Feelings,
Plucking the cords of my symphony!
No rhythm; No tone? Sounds escape me!
Am I confused? Hum... Somehow inside... Changes occurring;
The myth of evolution's in my mind! Released on Tuesday;
Jacket and all... Back on Wednesday; For what? I forgot...
Forgot what? Something else.

LONNIE E. TROTT

The Mirror In Me

10-31-94

Why don't you smile?
When you stare into me?
For if you could shine;
And glare like me,
What would you be?
Sincerely...!
Yes... I know your thoughts;
So don't even attempt, to smear me.
Yet than again, if you did;
What would you still see?
Reflecting?

LONNIE E. TROTT

34.

Self - Assurance

11-15-94

Cannot ye fly wingless, my little bird?
Will not try thee for fear the earth meet with?
Succeed the capable... Doith not for stage sanding!
Thy pride liveth for failure; your ability precedith with.

LONNIE E. TROTT

Inescapable

11-15-94

Peace within my mind, dreams grow.
Her heart's full of steam;
Yet with all that she brings,
Her journey's sure to go.
Freshly coated, her youth...
Yes, youth becomes her;
A scent to provocative to demise.
Like the path to my dreams on a rainbow ride...
Her eyes; from the light on that night, as snow.
Yes, she came with a goal to enlighten my soul.
Though the hurdle in my present's my stand.
As a river she flowed; with depth in every way,
Even granted, our destiny was, preplanned.

LONNIE E. TROTT

Never Promised

11-15-94

Beauty is as beauty does;
The eyes reflect the minds prospect.
Like a lost soul begets a world of confusion,
As ones heart ignites a spark for changes.
Like living, being, is a part of life;
Balanced with death; as loaned is to all...
Our existence.

LONNIE E. TROTT

Set Back

11-15-94

I can't stand losing my thoughts for my actions;
Slain to misery, my engine's without.
The Mask!
All channels meeting at a point;
A chipped edge deforming its slice...
My master's power I follow not.
The winged things gliding pass my fortress...
I believe, I believe now I've lost reasoning...
Please, please, please...!
Help me?

LONNIE E. TROTT

38.

Secret Affairs

11-17-94

I'm asked to poeticize her cup...
Hot tea filled, sweet 'n' low, No! Honey...
On my way, I wondered; his reason; his motive;
I stop...
Why should I serve his bidding? It's funny...
Am I being tested; or is he just smitten?
It's like "who done it", the smooth plot.
As I'm walking in... All eyes are fixed; on me;
The steam from my hand; or the sudden noise?
Just Shock... Yes...
Then I present; and accept an ardent smile.
Next I sit...
Then, from my left, a witty chuckle
As she nursed her sup.
And for him, her response;
To the essence, of what she held;
In her cup.

LONNIE E. TROTT

Welfare

11-20-94

At age cometh soon... My peak.
What have I to show, of my wares?
Fall's around the corner?
So too are all the rays;
And my flash to that of leaves drained;
Weakness not a fault...
A white sheet's wrinkle, Goeth the hour.
How must I hold? My clouds know no weight;
A grip in time lost late, never sooner.
Accepting all colors;
Cashing in wilt not lend a rainbow.
My core lest not a structure;
Or field,
Nor land,
Or Power!

LONNIE E. TROTT

40.

A Blink Of An Eye

12-05-94

They travel in units,
Tens and infrequently hundreds free.
Eluding the nets and traps all to be
Sometimes displayed for the intellectuals vainly.
So colorful in three; black, white and grey;
A velvety rainbow lest,
The sun sets back off their necks and fades away.
Such a cured sight for sad eyes like mine;
As they bathe in rays right at this time...
And not too pleasing,
Acknowledging this highbrow, structure along the path.
They soared to flight for fright of this sight;
Only too vague for my reasoning.
Come-back little friends, don't leave me?
Come-back!
My miseries once high; now low,
Shows hop, and promises, for a new day;
Tomorrow.

LONNIE E. TROTT

To Befriend A Stranger

12-11-94

Never lose sight of things held strong.
You give many: peace and hope.
Unaware of life's reason,
And paths taken right;
Side-a-facts of consumed knowledge wrong...
Sensing urges to act; make stand your goals firm!
Lost or won, still a champion.
Triumphs overcome, the miseries of my woe's
Concerning peace, like sunshine, as one.
Chance things anew! Dark dreams, blue;
Cause all that's told me,
Your Future's someone's
Too.

LONNIE E. TROTT

Never Lose Sight

12-14-94

Thirteen months made all the difference worth it.
Fourteen never had a meaning or tear.
Today's for hope. Apply your dreams, seize it.
Tomorrow's, still tomorrow, yet, a New Year!

LONNIE E. TROTT

Fulfillment From Within

12-14-94

In and out, the world goes round;
Never be too vain and Lose sight.
Now and then, our family lingers afar...
Love forever sustained... today: tomorrow:
What's to make of yesterday?
Ninety-three was bright...
Time has moved, within strong hearts;
Though off and on fades away.
To start; catch up!
For ninety-four is on the run;
Clouds full as foam-white and moving.
Then a soothing ninety-five brings love for all;
Tamed to rejoice the part.
Together, we are one; never shall we fall...
Cause within our hearts our house is right,
A Home.

LONNIE E. TROTT

44.

Liberative Nourishment

12-18-94

For my love, showing all that's precious;
Take me, as no other's been able,
Revealing parts, unhitched by the cable.
You only brighten, what's not luminous;
Too long, my miseries been ominous.
I want to be free; free and capable.
As a wild horse; unleashed from his stable.
Quick fast with unforces hands, spontaneous!
Is not that too, so much to ask my love?
Must my tongue freeze at thought of your calling?
Requesting little, lest thy glove fit not;
Feeling lower than dirt; man, I am falling...
Hope and courage, is all that is needed.
Take hold of thy life; what's lacking...
Feed It.

LONNIE E. TROTT

45.

Escaping Corruption

12-18-94

Fast and without thought;
One lash, bit the whip.
Why've I been cured?
That I should hear to this tone?
I'm just a loner; a bark for a bone.
To backlash me; a penalty, you'll strip!
Leak answers only, confirming our tip.
What, can I say? If recalling's not hone?
My rights keep failing why, owing gossip?
The vigils were amiss; yet my eyes held...
Sounds desperate from lips, to ears, my guess.
I'm the regal here; this case shall unfold!
Just being, that which mirrors yourself, pest.
You are you! And I am still; still in charge!
What are you doing?
Hey wait!!!
Man At Large!

LONNIE E. TROTT

Choices Evolved

12-18-94

Fly Away, Go...
To flight sets you freedom.
Home's where you belong;
True your kin awaits...
Don't look back, the traps forever open;
Rays of sparkled colors upon their gates.
Grasp what's true to you;
Not that which you hate.
Balance past experiences, with things new...
Dreams are twofold: your destiny and your fate.
It's true, the future evolves from your present too.
Yet, whatever your choices,
I'll Always LOVE YOU.

LONNIE E. TROTT

47.

Family Of Ninty-Four

12-19-94

Touching hearts in many ways; you are blessed.
Your strength and determination shows all;
From Lonnie and Andre, honoring your call...
Exuding your goodness, challenged to test;
Equality, you taught first, we were brushed.
Koolridge and Winslow attentive and wise,
Individually accepting their best.
Kevin and Leslie, all ears and eyes flushed;
Longing to blossom, from depths low to rise.
Christine Phillips, you're separate from the rest...
All and all, you've brought Joy to the assembly;
With one correction...
Never more a group;
We Are a Family.

LONNIE E. TROTT

48.

Angels Appear, In Many Forms

12-22-94

Vision never held peace, drive or plain sight;
Longing for serendipity, I'm blue.
Why must a dream come so now and so true?
Held in ones thoughts... They linger,
As this night some go.
Don't want to be lost; show me bright?
Holding all vocals, till no more... Hey, shoo!
Is this heart really calling? Calling you?
As I sleep; given into dusk... No! Light...
Let tomorrow bring joy; and things prized best.
Feeling cool; a balance within my reach.
Allow me solace; gifts of truce, and rest.
Permit this pleasure, without sound or breach?
I ask and tell all not for comfort or a stand.
Yet, so that, once open... Soaring through skies,
Beyond many a sea;
I'll always have my friend,
Or ear,
Near Me.

LONNIE E. TROTT

Hear Me

12-31-94

Like Beast...
Trapped In my own habitation.
Nowhere to run or contemplate,
A secluded bush.
Alone in thy shrub hole,
Though eyes... staring...
Like the owl, quite, in my stalk,
Nocturnally at peace.
A moon comes, like stars go;
Remote, in their starring...
Bright at dusk, gone come dawn;
How, how many more?
Never will light, nor wind or rain,
Brush thy gate.
Like yawning, breath or crying;
Natures evolving gifts.
As men, chained
To a nightmares dream!
Wanting to awake...
Every turn emitting tranquility;
Alas in transit, to a blankets charm.
While isolation begets thy fortress;
This nucleus breeds nerves
And sundry vacancies,
Yet I'm always busy.
Longing for rainy days
Lest a morning or noon
Deny thy evening.

Refusing these sad eyes rest.
As a final wish; summit thee sleep?
Thy blood as thy spirit
Sustaining thy journey...
No train can move; plane to fly;
Ship sail a sea for the need
Of thy soul to be free!
Take thee in arms;
Hold thy bone for luck?
For thou art decaying
Insight of changes.
Let a piece of thy being
Remaineth...
For thy mind is weak.
I know not what I mean!
Just sounds...
From noises...
A Whisper.

LONNIE E. TROTT

50.

Deship's Out Of Control

12-31-94

Take hold Pon De Wheel...
Touching veins of passion,
For no flame nor spark
Shall smother.
Come close, yet closer;
Feel my blood flowing?
Hypnotizing hearts like no other...
Sensing your freshness;
Young loins and all,
Tenderly, melting, your flesh.
Tasting all portholes;
Sweet oval treats.
Dancing and prancing,
Than splash!
As we meet,
Literally speaking;
Our bodies retreating...
One more Time;
Two full yokes;
Pon De Stash.

LONNIE E. TROTT

51.

Crawling Expeditiously

01-13-95

The vessel,
For far too long,
Has deny my flash.
The passing of time,
Eluding pain.
Above and beyond,
A swell ripples,
Expending, engaging,
That yet, to be confronted...
There's a need for my misery'
So, so many channels.
Though for me,
My destiny's my salvation.
I'm in sight of a vision;
A vision of cause.
For this reason,
Deduction's on the horizon.
On this day, misty clouds lay rest;
While sunshine constantly,
Baffles the rain.
I've seen twinkling many stars,
No need counting.
Behold,

A picture, its beauty mounted.
Just thinking, not wondering;
It all will come clear.
Take time for a cure...
Not Corruption.

LONNIE E. TROTT

Harmony

01-29-95

I've known,
What cleansing clean,
Dirt had smeared me.
A lapse in mind,
Judge not, my faults
Not so... Can I reason?
No thought shall hold,
Acts gone bye,
Will they, lest this season?
As true, a bubble pops,
Wash thy sea.
In tides I see past...
I'm a young ripple,
On bodies deep.
Will a rule
Thunder, in this open air?
Let nature sleep.
Forever warmed, by the sun...
Though for balance,
Give me rain...
For I'm now at peace,
Within my senses;
As a field,
Flows with grain.

LONNIE E. TROTT

I Am

01-29-95

What has life given?
That I can call my Own;
I'm so small...
For its freshness; accept Blue.
Your hearts feels, mind Wonders;
A journey shall partake.
Why not red; for its Strength...
Aide my pump, clear fog Web;
Vow never a Mistake?
What do you want? You've the gift of Life,
You have it All.
To have Freedom; as a bird in its Flight...
Never to Fall...
You can accomplish Wisdom.
Take your time, and Listen...
For you may lose, what's at Stake.
The world is Lost. This can't be true?
For there's something... Amiss.
Help me find it, knowing my Wrongs;
Show thee light, in thy Mist?
Revolutions reveal many Wonders.
Trust in truths Right... You're kindling.
I can feel it, it's in my Soul;
The warmth of a Great Fist.
Communicate your Weakness and pray...
Seeing Visions, if you're willing.
He will never forsake you; you are His Son.
Praise-God's-Name, for you are now Flying!

Soaring with Spirits; A soul, full of Joy.
Arise, with your Children... Almighty!
I'm longing to Worship, Only You, only You;
You, my One, and only You.
There's No "other" God, Only You, only You;
You, my One, and only You.
In Your hands, I Am, I'll do as You "Will".
You are My Lord; My Savior... Almighty!
I've found what I'd Lost; Misplaced, so to speak;
My-Faith-In-You, My Lord... Almighty!
From days gone by as this;
to those by Your Will to come...
My peace of mind, body and Soul,
Is endowed, by only You;
You, my One and only...
Lord Jesus.

LONNIE E. TROTT

In The Shadow, Of Gemini

02-12-95

Knowing the scent of Roses, in many a Garden;
Taking for granted our Seasonal senses... Love.
Above and beyond, without Time,
Can I sleep till tomorrow?
Could importance be outside of self...? Hate.
Wait! Wanting just to hold your hand... Silk.
Soothing miseries, inside my mind;
No charm cures a wondering man as thee... Glove.
As a dove, my loneliness within this World.
Retaining all sanity; a joy ones family shall gladly partake.
A headache sends me retreating. No!
Fleeting from darkness; embracing new Light.
The myth of all we want; yet, without its meaning.
I stand to reason; with love, not hate;
Within a glove, longing to partake.
Tomorrow,
Tomorrow...
Seeks Answers.

Lonnie E Trott

55·

Aiding Such A Basic

02-21-95

Tapping the power shows thirst, hope and light;
So many circuits all shades of white.
Can I feed breathe, for this day lost then?
Upon a ship, swells way high, and-still searching.
Nightly chills on my mind, wanting to see,
So Full... Wanting to go, to be free;
Holding me close... You know, by the moon, save a Sea...
Never foggy? Nah! It's not what I sense holding, strength there.
Behold, a vision, and sounding all trumpets... Clear!
Answers, answers, the answer's always been...
It wasn't far; not even deep, hey! It's, it's within:
A want... A need... to pray for my soul.
Forgiving those in misery; accepting God, ten-fold.
I thank you for caring; I believe in your heart.
You've shined on my tomorrow
Always unconditionally,
From the Start.

Lonnie E Trott

56.

Learning Inspired For Evolution

02-15-95

Time's my only friend;
In this world of yesterday.
I eat, sleep, and awake
In preparation for this day.
Why even this very minute,
Follows an oppression
From over four-hundred years lost.
My hour's now, to make a stand;
Live still then, and cry at every woe;
I don't think so!
I'm my own boss... Man!
There's so much blame,
To what can't be changed late.
Unaware of tomorrow,
I hold my head high,
And independent still,
Lend a helping hand.
As individuals,
A segment to that whole.
We take for granted
The fragrance of roses;
Fearing their uniqueness,
Their freshness, their smiles.
Our perceptions longs short,
To their golden display.
We're such a self-righteous people,
In this land so full of dept.
Why should I adhere?

To a renegades past stand?
I've been there and now still,
My eyes rain...
In pieces, my mind thunders
With utter blindness;
Lightning grazed my heart.
The way, this is not.
Experience is our history.
The future should be our gold.
Now's the time for healing,
And forgiving;
Some sincere soul searching.
Let's Praise God's Name...
By His Son....
Amen.

Lonnie E Trott

Schedule

02-29-95

Welcome, welcome...
To a den of one;
Not by chance
Though my bed is done.
Never a wrinkle on my cot,
Watched many stars
Leave the gentle sleeper.
A blissful peace like what?
To anticipate
The next changing keeper.
Locking off the passing time;
Through heavy windows
My eyes fooled not.
As I await
My appetite roars now.
I'm in need of fuel
To sustain my growl.
Closing in on seven
The hour's sure to come,
While the light starts breaking;
Longing for a rooster's call,
Praising nature's gifts
Under heaven.
Let all rejoice:
Big, slim, short and tall.
As they walk stiff,
Down through the hall...
Prior was dusk

Slowly fading anew...
As I breathe in life,
The sky and sea
Blend complete;
Watching shadows
Chasing this,
Catching that and you.
The keepers change on beat;
A click, a click
Then a click at my door.
Soon the pack to roam and bore.
How blue and on cue
My battle now to retreat.
Yawning,
Stretching,
Releasing...
To Sleep.

Lonnie E Trott

My Little Angel

03-05-95

There's light at every corner,
Warmer to those who seek;
Speaking feelings from my heart,
True, blue within my mind...
And hopeful.
Signs to guide me Home
A spark in case I need...
Feeding my spirit with understanding;
Withstanding, not, my scars that bleed.
You've touched strings which breathe me;
My fuel's bubbling with Joy...
I thank you.
For as long as I'm breathing and
My thoughts of you keep singing...
I'll be praising The Almighty God,
For our meeting

Lonnie E Trott

59.

Hallelujah

03-06-95

To God,
The Creator,
The Father...
The Almighty provider of Breath;
We hold Thee and Honor all matter
Your touch displays.
So much to believe in yet,
So few take notice...
For the Destroyer's hand's at work.
Oh Death!
Awaken from your dreams,
As God calls His Salvationers...
Bestowing light, governing our sight,
Longing for us to summit,
To His Righteous Way...
Direction, goals, motivation-
Growing Strong, around life's courses,
We're maturing.
Delegating strength among His Children;
Only one step need be taken;
Open our hearts and minds to God,
Who saved our sinful souls, by Jesus.
Praise Him,
Do not forsake Him...
Sing songs, sing His Name...
Lord Jesus.

Lonnie E Trott

Wings

03-12-95

Show me the way; way, way home;
And I will follow you there.
I'm a child in your hands;
Hold me, mold me;
Your touch so gentle
Because you care.
Blessed I am,
To have your time;
Granted not,
For I shall waste.
In favor of tomorrow
Should it come, or part in haste...
I'll cherish your heart's sublime.

Lonnie E Trott

61.

Father!!! I've Missed You!

05-05-95

Blessed,
In view of the fact,
That today the Almighty answered.
One of many,
Yet one more than none,
The "Farmer" arrived.
Through my foliage,
I've longed to sparkle,
Albeit, reality shaded-upon
My innocent youth's blind existence,
While, passing "Suns"
Constantly beat all day...
The previous night's moon,
Fed my roots, concurrently,
Maturing my stalk.
An exotic Osmund I am;
Study my language,
The "Wind" taught.
Yes, this day's to heal,
My ominous scars...
Unseen, unheard,
Unwanted I believe, I hid...
Hiding or blocking,
From what was never spoken,
Or questioned, till now.
Just the farmer and I;
For the "Field" was not summoned.
Bending now to my left...

Next, to my right...
Soon joining all our elements
To breathe as one;
Their mix, we'll bind.
An exotic Osmund I am;
Beauty smiles...
Blushing, my petals,
Almond.

Lonnie E Trott

62.

Our Rainbow

06-03-95

Though an ominous regret
Wishes not.
Another "Ten",
Weared its way home.
Our grey skies forever misty;
Will the sea flood the seeds?
You have grown?
All our sprouts
In their vast forms swaying;
A storm's call
Skillfully swarming our demise.
Oh prior,
To your sparkling warm eyes closing;
Cast a moon,
Upon thy stems,
Or a Ray.

Lonnie E Trott

63.

Family Of Ninety-Five

06-03-95

Christine...
Over expressive months,
You've caressed, nurtured,
Allowed us to envision reality;
The importance we and society
As a whole, take for granted.
Those little, yet individual attributes
Flowering within us;
Like life... Giving;
As the sun... forever shining;
To the stars... eternally winking;
From your smile,
A painted picture in our minds.

MAY YOUR AURA BREATH THAT "THREE"
WHICH WE WISH YOU:
LOVE, PROSPERITY,
AND HAPPINESS.

Lonnie E Trott

64.

Revealing The Evolution Of Nature

06-01-95

Energy, space...
All existing matter;
The universe.
Mankind's world...
A planet of lost
And wounded creatures;
Earth...
A baby, a child, a teen...
Then call themselves;
Responsible.
Yet, they allow
Pride, and precedence over
Their Divine characteristics,
Warring within them.
Do people not realize?
That they are;
Beautiful; strong; meek?
They are, unique.
Yet again, like life,
They take for granted
What's been given!
They look to impress others...
Gradually shrinking,
Devaluing their strength,
Their humbleness, forgotten.
Unique...
What do you think?
They long for today;

For tomorrow's tomorrow.
All that they have; do they need?
Do they give? Do we share?
It's me, me, mine and I.
Choices...
Individually unique, we are;
And choices, we have.
But that day will come, when,
We all will be as one:
No more prejudice...
But abundantly
Sensitive fellowship.
God's Gift is, the "light";
The "Truth",
Salvation.
It's for you...
It's for me...
It's for us...
Our Family.

Lonnie E Trott

Sparkles

07-10-95

Over lost years,
I'd lost your vision;
Too long, yet long enough,
I settled.
We've joked, we've laughed.
We have talked, we are fine;
Separated by life's courses
Through time.
Though I'd wondered for so long;
If I'd been forgotten as an old song
Or until one day, as this day,
When we'd grown.
I was so pleased by your coming,
To visit... I smiled;
And still gleaming,
From a distance of many miles.
So keep on sparkling, over my nights;
For the Lord, governs our light.
You're a scented rose,
In the world.
What a sight!

Lonnie E Trott

66.

My Friend

08-08-95

From the beginning of life;
My time was shielded, protected.
Unaware, for I knew not, what was...
Absorbing your precious love.
Always giving...
You, held my hand; just because.
Cause warmth your arms gave,
Saved many a tears, when I was "blue".
Giving, mending "our" broken hearts,
We bless you.
I thank you, for all your nurturing,
Guidance and understanding.
I'll treasure every thought and moment,
Housed in memory.
You are now freedom, flying high,
To the Son, He heard your cry...
For his love, for His grace,
And for all, that He is...
My Wessy;
My Friend...
The Air which I Feed.

Lonnie E Trott

Themes

Family	Hope	A Mom's greatest joy
Cater-Cousin	Romance	Giving friend
The Picture	Romance	The Strength of Passion
Focus	Hope	My Strength is my Weakness...
You You	Romance	A Light at the End
Where's the Light?	Friendship	Took for Granted
Endurance	Frustration	The Power in Hope
Reality	Hope	Priceless Smile
Tipped	Flirty	Possible Possibilities
Foresight	Wisdom	Know your Limits
A chance	Flirty	No Bridge to Wide
Evolution (1)	Flirty	Emotions do Win
Evolution (2)	Change	Positive Healing
Evolution (3)	preparation	Breaking Barriers
Precious 70th	Bonding	No Greater Emotion
Perfection	Friendship	This is My Name
Unsettled	Wisdom	Can't Escape what's Yours
What, Where, to Why & How	Wisdom	Not Always a Peach
Life	Change	Time to Reboot
Forgiveness	Wisdom	Dared, to Take a Step
Yes & No	Wisdom	Unity
Try Something Divergent	Flirty	Honesty is Key
Soul Searching	Wisdom	At Face Value
Awaken	Frustration	Nowhere to Hide
Which Way	Confusion	Bomb Defused
Home	Fulfillment	Inner Strength
Diablo's Misfortune	Hope	A Chance
Lean on Me	Romance	Enough is Enough
Personality	Playful	The "Think Tank"

Hallelujah	Change	Give The Lord
Wings	Hope	High Regards For...
Father!!! I Missed You	Change	Direct Trust... Heals
Our Rainbow	Family	Missing Granny
Family of Ninety-Five	Friendship	Remembered Seeds
Revealing The Evolution Of Nature	Wisdom	On Our Way Home
Sparkles	Friendship	My Heart beat Sparked
My Friend	Friendship	A Grandson's Jewel

Printed in the United States
By Bookmasters